THERE IS

GOLD

IN YOUR

GOAL

LEWIS DRAZ ASBURY SR.
Author of *From Start Date, To Start Up*

There is
GOLD
in your
GOAL

Written by Lewis DraZ Asbury
Edited by Brandi Starkey

Published in the United States by DraZ Creative Marketing, LLC and DraZ Creative Works

Subjects: Success | Entrepreneurship | Goal Setting | Planning

Cover Design: DraZ Creative Marketing, LLC

Intro

Sports & Entertainment

On The Job

Your Business

Personal Goals

Final Thoughts

Worksheet

Intro

As kids, I think between Kindergarten & 1st Grade,
we get asked that age old question;
"What do you want to be when you grow up?"
Let's be honest for a minute. Who actually knows at
that age what they want to be? How many of us
grow up and become that?
I know my son probably won't grow up to be
Batman. Or maybe he will.
Even still, I encourage his enthusiasm and vision to
become a superhero, because
I know that superheroes come in many forms.

I began this book with that in mind, as it pertains to
our goals. Our coming into adulthood and
thereafter. Our lives become full of things. Things
we want, things we want to experience, things we

want to have. All of those things seem unrealistic, until we begin to put them on paper.

Many of those things can be very beneficial to our lives, but we hold them captive in fear. In my position as a graphic designer and business consultant, I come across a hundreds of people who have ideas. There's always that initial excitement about their new idea. Then comes the tremble in their voices & the poorly disguised uncertainty. The fear barriers.

"Where do I start?"
"What will people think?"

The room of success becomes brighter once we look outside the walls that keep us content. When you're in your bedroom, it's dark. Your bed is comfortable. Your pillow is soft and your comforter is warm. Keyword; "comforter". If you step outside of your bed, open your blinds or curtains to a sunny day, you'll find that your room is instantly brightened, and that is a light shining on your "comforter". Apply that visual to your goals. If you move that comforter or cover to the side, let your foot hit the floor and your first steps and to move forward with your day, you're also taking one step towards your goal.

We now live in a time where the internet, more directly, social media consumes us. Many of us are guilty of being sucked into and consumed by lives of those we follow. With that being said, it's important that we follow those who will add value to our lives, not those who will decrease that value. Quality over Quantity.

Sports & Entertainment (Lifestyle)

Rapper and Mogul Jay Z said in a verse on his joint album with his wife, Beyonce, "Here we say you broke if everybody is broke except for you". The break down of that phrase simply means, "you are the company you keep." If your timeline or newsfeed is populated with individuals who constantly party, drink, smoke, have multiple sexual partners, etc., you're subconsciously programming your mind & glorifying the behaviors. Why not adjust yourself and your surroundings to accommodate the successful life you truly want to live?

If you come from a lower class neighborhood, and you take one of the opportunities that we all have to be successful, your surroundings will change according to your success. You will adjust your lifestyle to your new standards of living. That brand new car that you've dreamt about and can now afford, will suddenly not look as good sitting outside of that same home, in that same neighborhood. That new home you purchase, will begin to not look as appealing with an old beater in the driveway. If you are a social person like myself, you may begin attending events that your current circle of friends think is too much for them. Those things force change. No one works as hard as they do to stay the same, or to remain stagnant.

NBA player and mogul, Lebron James, is one of the most current and relevant examples. He began his career in one position, as a base. That base formed a mold as he became comfortable with how everyone plays. There's that comfort word again. Once he reached a certain level, he desired more experience. Lebron took a trade opportunity that placed him in Miami. That gave him the opportunity to first Learn, then remove the "L" so that he could Earn. His transition caused some upset to dedicated fans. They did not understand, nor did they want to accept the business move. But Lebron was up to something.

After gaining that experience in Miami, he took the tools and insight he gained back to Cleveland and helped his home team advance to higher levels. Consequently, he increased his own personal value. It's like home improvement. You purchase a home or property, fix it up and then sell it for more with the new increased value. Lebron hit the market again signing a new deal at $154mil. It was a no brainer against his then $99mil at home. Men lie, women lie, numbers don't. In my opinion that's pretty smart. Once you begin to know your worth, the ball (in this case), is in your court.

The goal in sports is more than just the field goal. It's about how much money & how big of an impact you can make, doing what you love. At the end of the day it's a business, the same as any other and every business has goals to work towards.

On The Job

No matter what industry you're in, there are tools in place to help ensure that goals are met throughout the business. Call centers have call handling metrics, fast food restaurants have speed of service times they measure, and all businesses have direct financial goals to obtain. They have even more goals that apply towards company growth. On every job interview that I've ever been on, I've been asked one common question, "Where do you see yourself in 5 years?" Many times I've wanted my response to be, "not here" but of course, the question was based on your career goals. They're looking for a couple of things with that question, but mostly they want to know if you're a person of growth or a person of comfort.

Usually I would answer as seeing myself in the interviewers position, given that they are a part of management or an executive of some sort. I've gotten some chuckles with that response.I would further clarify & ensure that it was not to replace them, but to walk in their path as my leader, assuming that they would grow as well. Setting a goal for yourself on the job, aside from the goals of the company, is imperative. Whatever you do, don't give up until you reach that goal. No one is impressed by, or remembers the person who quit, or came in second. We all remember the person who worked hard to become number one and set new records. If you are working for a company that has growth opportunities available, set aside some time within your first week to look at the company profile or intranet for internal job postings. If there are none available at that time, check back periodically. Have a goal set in your mind that you have 90 days to show and prove. In reference to the previous chapter, adding value to yourself gives you the upper hand.

Setting that goal for yourself will align your focus and your drive. WRITE IT DOWN! Consider a personal calendar to countdown the days or a journal where you can note your day to day growth and accomplishments towards reaching that goal. If you miss a day where you did not take a step greater than the previous, don't worry. It's alright. Everyday is a new opportunity, however; do not make everyday a repeat of the previous day and keep telling yourself that you can try again tomorrow. POSITIVE STEPS! You have to take inspired action and create positive change. That is the power you have over your mind. Once you come to that realization, you will find the strength and will to progress daily.

I was once in a position making an excellent salary, but that was only after I took the steps previously mentioned. I came into a company as a contract/temporary employee. In less than 90 days, I applied for a permanent position and got it! 60 days later, another opportunity came about where a coworker wanted to advance, but had no one willing to take her current position. Guess what? I applied again. After working that new position for a year, I decided to take it a step further and apply for a position which required me to relocate to another state. The new position already had a candidate identified, but because I had applied, as protocol, they had to interview me. I walked into the interview with three levels of recommendations. The first was from my direct manager. The second was from the department supervisor, and the final one was from the regional director.

With those three letters in hand, I was granted the opportunity. Why? They all noted one common quality; I was goal driven.

Your Business

Why do we go into business for ourselves?

It's simple; You want to run your own show. You'll never meet someone as hungry as you about your goals. Take control of your dream!

Everyone has a talent of some sort. Many of us turn that talent into an active hobby. If you are REALLY passionate or knowledgeable about something, why not perfect it and turn it into a paycheck? As I, and many others have said, the average successful person has multiple streams of income. Your talents can and should be one of them. As an employee, you should never get comfortable, and reliant on your income as your sole base of living. At any moment it, all of it can be taken away from you. Everyone should have both passive and active incomes.

Passive Income is income received on a regular basis that usually requires little or no work to generate it. Examples are; rental property, network marketing, stocks or anything you invest in, that will continually work for itself.

Active Income is income received from performing a service, such as a job.

When I started my own company, DraZ Creative Marketing, LLC., I was a full time employee during the day and at night, I was up creating and fulfilling design orders. After several years, I did reach a point where I felt business was steady enough to replace my employment income. As mentioned in my previous book, *From Start Date, To Start Up*, I took a leap of faith and quit my job to run my business full time. After doing so and facing many challenges, I learned that the leap was premature. I had not set and stayed concrete to a goal. I would often tell myself, and sometimes to this day, I still say that we do not need motivation, we need discipline. Our friend Webster defines discipline as: activity or experience that provides mental or physical training. Both goal setting and discipline are cornerstones of personal achievement.

Here are 8 Key Disciplines In Running A Business:

1. Start with an ongoing customer focus.
One of the quickest ways to fail in business, is to allow your passion for a solution to convince you that everyone will want one.

Don't assume anything until you have done market research and listened to real customers. Then, assume the customers will change over time. NEVER STOP LISTENING!

2. Create a specific and detailed business plan.
A successful business requires focus. Define the customer need with a specific solution for a specific price and cost. Normally the goal is to make enough money to be sustainable and provide a return on the investment of constituents.

A written plan is helpful for communication to others

3. Construct a team with the right skills and experience.

Most experts agree that a great team is more important than a great product.

The ideal team includes at least one expert on the solution, and at least one experienced business person. Together they set the standard for collaboration and culture that will make or break the company.

4. Treat every business dollar as a personal one.

New business owners are often quick to spend outside investment funding, and quick to delegate money management to accountants in the business.

Successful entrepreneurs are more likely to fund their own business, and use the discipline of personally validating and approving every payment.

5. Learn to communicate effectively.

People can't work for you if they don't know what you expect, and the message has to be updated and communicated daily. This was an initial fault of mine while expanding.

Customers and partners won't find you or buy from you if you can't tell them why, how, what they need, and what you offer.

Communication must be proactive, not reactive.

6. Demonstrate an ongoing sense of urgency.
In today's world, the market evolves even faster than the technology. Time is of the essence in everything you do.

The business race is not a sprint. There is no finish line. Learn to enjoy the journey as well as the destination.

7. Manage the business with metrics and goals.

Working hard is necessary, but not sufficient enough alone, for success. Business objectives need to be listed and measured to assess progress and positioning against competition.

Metrics drive a results-oriented culture. That, in turn, leads to continuous quality improvements, pivot points, and recognition of success along the way.

8. Build mental strength and resilience.

Every business encounters unanticipated obstacles. Those due to economic conditions, natural disasters or competitor challenges. Start practicing resilience early, so that you can recover quickly when needed.

One of the most common reasons I see for startup failure is that the entrepreneur gives up too early, rather than fight through these challenges.

I know first hand that starting and growing a business is hard. It is at least as difficult as developing an innovative solution.

The difference is that developing a new solution typically requires specialized skills, creative thinking, and strong passion. Starting a business is more about planning, disciplined actions, and problem solving.

Don't lose the race halfway to the finish line.

Personal Goals

Focus on your goal and do not look in any direction but ahead. If you must look back, only do so to check your progress. Keep going forward. Our personal goals are what keep our ego and self confidence in tact. When thinking about your personal goals, it is important to set ones that you can achieve. Everyone else (employers, parents, society) will set unrealistic goals for you. They will often do this in ignorance of your own desires and ambitions.

I recently had a conversation with someone who stated they did not feel any progression in their life. Although, they had several businesses meeting and exceeding in goals, a family, great group of friends, what more can one ask for? It's lonely at the top is a quote that comes to mind as I've heard several rappers and successful entrepreneurs mention time and time again. One can have it all, and nothing at the same time. I asked the person I was speaking to;

What are you working towards?

Do you have a goal in mind?

He replied: "Honestly, no I don't."

Following his responses, I simply advised him to:

1. Decide what you want.

2. Write it down.

3. Make a plan.

4. Work on it daily

Excuse my French, but you can't half-ass anything. Whatever you do, you have to REALLY do it, or not at all. Working and investing, without a goal in mind is clearly a half-ass attempt at being successful. As mentioned in my first book, *From Start Date, To Start Up*, working without a goal was my first failure in which led me back to full-time employment very quickly. The gentleman was feeling stagnant, although successes were present, because he did not have a clear view of his goal.

The only way to know what we want for our future and how we will get there, is to know where we are right now in life and in satisfaction. Share your vision with those you trust. When someone knows what your goals are, they hold you accountable. They'll question where you are in the process of achieving that goal. Accountability is the meat of the process. If a goal is set and only one person knows about it, it has no power. A goal holds no weight if you don't have one or more people who can hold you accountable to it.

When I began my first weight loss journey, some friends and I formed a group. One of the guys in the group asked me on my first day, what size I wanted to get down to. Then, I was between a XXL and XXXL in shirts (depending on the cut and fabric.) My reply was, XL. He told me that it would be easy, but that he would make me work for it. He kept his promise. There is a quote that says "Anything worth having is worth working for," or something similar to it. I knew that I wanted to give it a try. It had been over 5 years since I had seen the inside of a gym, and now that I had others holding me accountable for my goal, I couldn't back.

Changing my diet and daily routine were the disciplinary actions needed, in working towards my goal of a better me. One thing I noticed was the increased drive and energy I gained once I started eating better, working out daily and getting to sleep at a decent hour. Every goal should have a timeframe attached to it. One of the powerful aspects of a goal is that it has an end. A time that you are shooting to accomplish it in. I gave myself that same 90 days time-frame, as mentioned in *On The Job*. As time passes, you work on it because you don't want to get behind. You work hard because you want to meet that deadline. You may find it helpful to break down a huge goal into smaller goals with shorter timeframes. Mine as well as many others with fitness goals, were progress pictures. You MUST celebrate the small victories. Mission Accomplished!

The first step to setting personal goals that will bring you a successful life is to stop setting goals that will bring you a negative life.
Most goals are about a destination. "I want a million dollars." "I want happiness." "I want a new car." Try

instead to set your goals based on the journey. "What will make me happy?" "How can I work towards getting a new car?"

One step forward every day
Do something every day to move forward with your plan. Develop a habit of self-discipline and resolve to take at least one action each day on that one most valuable task, until it's complete. Again, it doesn't matter how small the task is, as long as there is daily progress towards your target. Some days you may take on bigger actions than others but, in taking **some** form of action, each and every day, you'll relentlessly chip away at your goal.

No progress is bad progress, so make a commitment to take daily action on the goal that will have the single biggest impact on your life. You'll be surprised at how much this simple approach will move you towards your goals quickly and effectively.

Final thoughts

Once your plan is set and you're taking daily action towards it, there are two important things you need to consistently do;

1. Keep track

Review your plan monthly as I did with my fitness journey. See how you're progressing towards your goals and tweak things as necessary. Don't put your plan into a drawer or hide it. Display it somewhere you will see it daily, to serve as a reminder.

2. Celebrate The Small Victories

Celebrate your successes by rewarding yourself if you complete a milestone for one of your goals. This can be anything you wish to grant yourself with in order to keep you motivated and inspired.

There is GOLD in your GOAL.

It is always too early to quit. Most people usually give up right before their breakthrough occurs.

Also available from the author:

Books of inspiration:

Russell Simmons - "Do You!: 12 Laws to Access the Power in You to Achieve Happiness and Success"
"Do You…" was the first book I started reading after maybe 5-6 years of not reading anything but social media, magazines and news clippings. I'd just folded my business in Atlanta and began transitioning back to Chicago. During that transition is when I also began my fitness journey as mentioned in this book, so it came right on time and definitely helped my physical and mental reconditioning.

Russell Simmons - "Super Rich: A Guide to Having It All"
After completing "Do You…" I moved on to "Super Rich…". Since I'd just taken such a loss by closing everything I was building in Atlanta, I felt the title, as well as Russell Simmons brand name is what

grabbed me. This being the 2nd book I picked up during my reconditioning period, Super Rich was in place to motivate me to keep pushing when I felt I should quit. Reassuring me that I am Super Rich, not monetarily, but mentally and in network.

Ash Cash - "The Wake Up Call: Financial Inspiration Learned from 4:44 + A Step by Step Guide on How to Implement Each Financial Principle"

Ash Cash served for me as an "Internet Motivator" I'd call it. I began following Ash Cash on instagram maybe around 2015-2016 as he'd post daily inspirational paragraphs and memes, a lot of which I began re-posting for myself and my own followers. Doing so is what got me into posting my own regular motivational statuses across the web that many know me for today. Me being a JAY-Z fan, purchasing this book was natural for me. JAY had just released his 4:44 album in which I completely felt, beyond being a fan, but the perspectives on culture it contained. When I caught wind that Ash wrote his own analysis, from a financial standpoint, it was a no brainer for me to grab and read cover to

cover. Between the album and the book, I'd taken a
new interest in financial freedom and started
changing my relationship with money.

Jeremiah J. Brown - "Financial Freedom: My Only
Hope"
As mentioned above, "Financial Freedom..." was a
spin from the JAY album so the title grabbed me,
especially since I'd taken a new interest in finance.
Jeremiah J. Brown gives a more raw perspective
on the banking and trade systems and how to
change your relationship with money in a way that it
should work FOR you.

Thank you!

I would like to say thank you to everyone who has followed me on social media over the years. As many of you know, I post and promote positivity on a regular basis, in attempt to balance out the negative energies many of those we follow, display.

Why is this book so short? Nowadays, I find it hard to capture a person's attention for a long period of time, and this test began with my social media quotes and posts over the years. Finding that, the longer the post, the less interaction we have, unless its a controversial topic of course. I truly hope that although short, each and everyone of you who read and/or purchased this book, gained something large from it. Again, I thank you.

Lewis DraZ Asbury Sr.

Worksheet

1. What is your goal?

   _____

   _____

   _____

   _____

2. Why is your goal important?

   _____

   _____

   _____

   _____

3. List potential problems that might keep you
   from completing your goal?

   _____

   _____

   _____

   _____

4. Goal completion date:_____

Action Item:

_____
_____Date_____
Action Item:

_____
_____Date_____
Action Item:

_____
_____Date_____
Action Item:

_____
_____Date_____
Action Item:

_____
_____Date_____
Action Item:

_____
_____Date_____
Action Item:

_____
_____Date_____